First
Facts®

FACT
FILES

U.S. GOVERNMENT

What You Need to Know

by MELISSA FERGUSON

CAPSTONE PRESS
a capstone imprint

First Facts are published by Capstone Press,
1710 Roe Crest Drive, North Mankato, Minnesota 56003
www.mycapstone.com

Library of Congress Cataloging-in-Publication Data
Library of Congress Cataloging-in-Publication data is available on the Library of Congress website.
ISBN 978-1-5157-8118-9 (library binding)
ISBN 978-1-5157-8129-5 (paperback)
ISBN 978-1-5157-8136-3 (eBook PDF)

Editorial Credits
Mandy Robbins, editor; Jenny Bergstrom, designer; Kelly Garvin, media researcher; Laura Manthe, production specialist

Photo Credits
Alamy Images/Kathy deWitt, 15; Shutterstock: Africa Studio, cover (bottom right), Andre Nantel, 5, Andrey_popov, 16, Billion Photos, backcover, Burlingham, 20, Everett-Art, 7, Everett Historical, 19, holbox, 3, Illerlok_Xolms, 13, JPL Designs, 11, Onur ERSIN, cover (top right), 9, Pakhnyushchy, 22, Rawpixel.com, 21, Steve Heap 10, STILLFX, cover (bottom left), tlegend, cover (top left), 1, trekandshoot, 17

Printed in China.
010295F17

Table of Contents

Government and You

A large group of people run the United States government. The government passes **laws**. Some laws keep you safe. Others protect your freedom.

In 1783 the Americans won the Revolutionary War (1775–1783). They were free of British rule. But their new nation needed rules. This is how the United States government began.

FACT
Americans celebrate their freedom on the 4th of July. This holiday is called Independence Day.

law—a rule made by the government that must be obeyed

Colorado Congress Chamber

AMERICAN REVOLUTION TIMELINE

The first battles of the
Revolutionary War take place.

1775

Battles are fought between the British
and Americans throughout the colonies.

1776–1783

Great Britain
admits defeat.

1783

1764–1774

A series of British laws
angers American colonists.

1776

American leaders create the Declaration of Independence.
It states that the United States is its own country.

The Founding Fathers

George Washington, James Madison, and Benjamin Franklin are three of America's Founding Fathers. These men helped create a strong government for the people. Each had a different role. George Washington was the first president of the United States. James Madison helped write the U.S. **Constitution**. Benjamin Franklin was a scientist, inventor, and writer. His ideas helped shape our government.

Constitution—a legal document that describes the basic form of the U.S. government and the rights of citizens

GEORGE

Washington

- lived 1732–1799
- U.S. president 1789–1797

BENJAMIN

Franklin

- lived 1706–1790
- U.S. ambassador 1776–1785

JAMES

Madison

- lived 1751–1836
- U.S. president 1809–1817

The Constitution

"We the People of the United States" are the famous first words of the Constitution. The Constitution is a plan for the government. It lists our country's rules and *citizens'* rights.

The Constitution became law in 1789. It formed the government the United States has today.

★★★ Constitution Day ★★★

Congress made Constitution Day a holiday in 2004. It is a day for Americans to remember what the Constitution says and how it affects our lives. Constitution Day is celebrated on September 17. This is the day the Constitution was signed in 1787.

PARTS OF THE CONSTITUTION

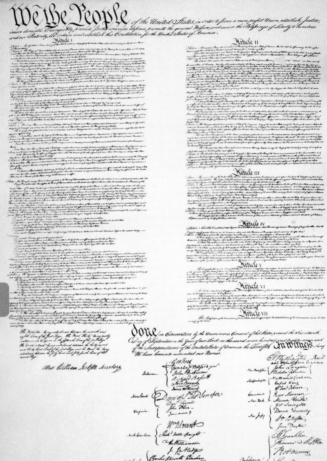

PREAMBLE

This part introduces the document and explains what the Constitution is for.

ARTICLES

The Articles explain the different parts of the U.S. government and what they do.

AMENDMENTS

The Amendments are changes and additions to the U.S. Constitution. They include the rights of all American citizens.

citizen—a member of a country or state who has the right to live there

How Our Government Works

We live in a democratic republic. People choose their own leaders in this type of government.

Our government has three parts. They are the legislative branch, the executive branch, and the judicial branch. The branches have the same amount of power.

THREE BRANCHES OF GOVERNMENT

CONSTITUTION
Provides a Separation of Powers

LEGISLATIVE

MAKES LAWS

EXECUTIVE

CARRIES OUT LAWS

JUDICIAL

EVALUATES LAWS

- ➤ Congress
  - ➤ Senate
  - ➤ House of Representatives

- ➤ President
  - ➤ Vice President
  - ➤ Cabinet

- ➤ Supreme Court
- ➤ Other Federal Courts

The Legislative Branch

The legislative branch is called Congress. Congress votes to make our country's laws. This branch is made up of two groups. They are the Senate and the House of Representatives.

Each state has two senators. They are **elected** every six years. Each state also has at least one representative. They are elected every two years. The number of representatives from each state depends on its **population**.

elect—to choose someone by voting
population—a group of people who live in a certain place
territory—an area under the control of a country but not part of that country

THE NUMBER OF
REPRESENTATIVES
IN EACH STATE

The Executive Branch

The executive branch of government carries out the laws. The president of the United States leads this branch. He is also in charge of the **military**.

The president does not work alone. He gets help from his vice president and **Cabinet**. The Cabinet gives the president advice.

military—the armed forces of a state or country
Cabinet—the president's group of advisers who are heads of government agencies

PRESIDENTS

PORTRAIT OF A PRESIDENT

QUALIFICATIONS

A president must be at least 35 years old. He or she has to be a natural-born citizen of the United States and a resident of the United States for at least 14 years.

TERM

Four years; can serve up to two terms.

HOME

The White House in Washington, D.C.

YEARLY SALARY

$400,000

JOB

Leader of the United States and head of the military. Works with foreign leaders on issues such as trade.

PROTECTED BY

Secret Service

The Judicial Branch

The courts make up the judicial branch. The judicial branch decides the meaning of laws when there are conflicts.

The Supreme Court is the head of the judicial branch. There are nine Supreme Court judges called justices. They rule on important court cases.

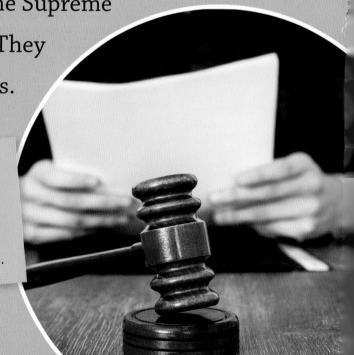

FACT

Sonia Sotomayor is the nation's first Hispanic Supreme Court Justice. She became a Supreme Court Justice in 2009.

U.S. Supreme Court

EQUAL JUSTICE UNDER LAW

Why We Need Laws

Everyone needs to follow the law. It is part of being a good citizen. Laws help keep people and places safe.

Laws can change over time. Many children worked in **factories** in the 1800s. It was dangerous work. In 1938 a law was passed that kept young children from working.

factory—the place where a product, such as a car, is made

Electing Leaders

Americans **vote** for their leaders in **elections**. When you turn 18, you can vote in government elections. Voting is a right of every adult citizen.

Government leaders make important decisions. Citizens vote for the people they think are best for the job. Leaders and citizens work together to make better laws.

vote—to make a choice in an election
election—the process of choosing someone or deciding something by voting

20

Glossary

Cabinet (KA-buh-nit)—the president's group of advisers who are heads of government agencies

citizen (SI-tuh-zuhn)—a member of a country or state who has the right to live there

Constitution (kahn-stuh-TOO-shuhn)—a legal document that describes the basic form of the U.S. government and the rights of citizens

democratic republic (de-muh-KRA-tik ri-PUHB-lik)—a form of government in which people vote for their leaders

elect (i-LEKT)—to choose someone by voting

election (i-LEK-shuhn)—the process of choosing someone or deciding something by voting

factory (FAK-tuh-ree)—a building where workers make goods

law (LAW)—a rule made by the government that must be obeyed

military (MIL-uh-ter-ee)—the armed forces who protect and defend a country

population (pop-yuh-LAY-shuhn)—the number of people who live in an area

territory (TER-uh-tor-ee)—an area under the control of a country but not part of that country

vote (VOHT)—to make a choice in an election

Read More

Harris, Nancy. *What's Government? First Guide to Government.* Revised Edition. Chicago: Heinemann, 2016.

Richmond, Benjamin. *What Are the Three Branches of Government? And Other Questions About the U.S. Constitution.* New York: Sterling Children's Books, 2014.

Worth, Bonnie. *One Vote, Two Votes, I Vote, You Vote.* New York: Random House, 2016.

Internet Sites

Use FactHound to find Internet sites related to this book.

Visit *www.facthound.com*

Just type in 9781515781189

Super-cool stuff!

Check out projects, games and lots more at
www.capstonekids.com

Critical Thinking Questions

1. What are the three branches of the U.S. government? What are they responsible for?
2. Can you think of a law you would like to see passed? What is it, and why do you think it's important?
3. What do you think is a good quality for a president to have? Why is that quality important?

Index

About the Author

Melissa Ferguson works for a corporate educational company that focuses on urban youth. She is a social studies content specialist and program coordinator. She also has experience as a senior editor and writer in the publishing field. She holds an MA in English from the University of St. Thomas in St. Paul, Minnesota. Besides writing, she enjoys finding "treasures" at flea markets and antique shops. She lives in a suburb of Minneapolis.